To a Teenage Soul

A poetry anthology for teenagers by a teenager

By Clementine Oliver

Front cover by Lui Ka

A DEDICATION

To my Family who always support me.

To my friends who encourage me.

To Lui Ka for the wonderful cover.

To Natalie, my brilliant editor.

Finally to teenagers who inspire me.

The ultimate rant from The Illustrator

I should never have accepted this commission.

Shackled by the stubborn self,
Entrapped by the evil bribery of a free subway,
Endeavoured to enchant.

To a Teenage soul.
How.
Exultant.

Letting off too much stream,
Is bad for your health they say.
Graceless paint brushes,
How dare you disturb my precious sleep.
Those who think I am too pessimistic read the first letter of every line.

Lui Ka

Contents

To a teenage soul	5	To the poor young pregnant girl	37
Eternally sober	6	Black	38
Please, help me escape	7	Rose petals	39
Examination contamination	8	Family	40
Boarding life	9	Homework	41
Crimson kiss	10	Graduation	42
Cyber day	11	English class	43
Daisy chain	12	What is healthy?	44
Demonstration of death	13	Northern lights	45
Fairy ring	14	For the last time	46
Form time	15	Pieces of broken glass	47
First snow	16	A flickering light	48
Late night taunts	17	Letting go	49
My friendship	18	Mistaken	50
My phone	19	A question	51
That night was beautiful	20	Lies	52
The heartless days	21	Misunderstood	53
To a ghost	22	Death penalty	54
Sports day	23	Just an outcast	55
Our actions	24	The dreaded phone call	56
Alone	25	Never to be forgotten	57
Maybe	26	Lightning strikes again	58
Midnight life	27	Time stops for no man	59
It will not happen	28	A flash of hope	60
Friday	29	A girl's night out	61
Summer days	30	Falling in love for the first time	62
Parent plot	31	The accident	63
Christmas day	32	City	64
Delightful bliss	33	Countryside	65
Prize giving	34	Story time	66
Size	35	Grow to care	67
Beauty	36	Lessons	68

To the unseen, millions misunderstood.

Oh, the carefree times we will soon leave.

A time of your life you can be yourself.

Terrifying years they are as well.

Every tear shed is memorable.

Every laugh is too.

No one can forget these eventful years.

And no one should forget.

Grownups should remember this time too.

Every time they see their children.

So in the meantime, my friends beware.

Of letting the dark come inside you.

Use your mind to keep you safe.

Light up the dark which comes from within.

I am eternally sober.

I do not drink.

I know the dangers.

I have seen what it does.

Drunks are good for nothing fools.

Flashing lights, a crowded room.

Friends surround me.

A glass is offered.

I refuse.

It is offered again.

What's the danger?

I don't refuse.

I tip the glass to my lip, down my throat it starts to drip.

I enjoy the feeling all too well

But I am eternally sober, for now anyway.

Please, help me escape.

I am always trapped.

I'm held in these halls.

I cannot escape.

It is too damn hard.

I have to just stay.

Live my days in bliss.

Let my hopes float away.

Float into the clear skies.

Clear to disappear.

EXAMINATION CONTAMINATION

Exams contaminate me.

They contaminate my thoughts, actions and words.

They invade my life.

The sounds fill your ears.

One sound is the scratching scurrying of pens.

Pages, slicing themselves apart.

They are an illness.

It leaves you tired, depressed.

With a decrease in the way you dress.

In the end it makes you stronger.

When the illness goes, the feeling of relief is dominant.

But also dread for the next examination contamination.

The dreams of boarding flick through my mind, all the things you hear in books.

Midnight feasts and much laughter, pranks, midnight feasts and food fights

All these are but dreams.

In reality?

There is affectionate waking up (with a video camera or piercing bell).

There are midnight feasts (of one square of chocolate).

There are pranks (which leave your room smelling).

There are food fights (which leave you hoovering orange).

Pillow fights which leave you winded.

One thing is that it is always busy.

When I see images of boarding life, they are always moving.

Bella who is bee lining for the backdoor.

Bianca is bouncing back from ballet.

The girls are swinging spiritedly.

After sermons at weekly mass.

Girls are jumping on their beds in the dorms.

Late night cleaning of rooms.

Miss T is scowling.

I am waiting quietly, suitcase in hand.

I am looking at the place which has been a home for seven solid years.

A tear rolls down my cheek.

It is the end of my boarding life.

The steel is cold.

It is deathly cold.

I feel the blade slide across my flesh.

It kisses my skin.

Molten red pulses from the slit.

The Crimson Kiss of the body.

Feelings surround my soul.

The gentle pain throbs.

It feeds the darkness.

It makes it bloom.

CYBER DAY

No adult understands it.

They live in fear of it.

Never knowing when it is going to happen.

All they know is that one day, every once in a while,

It happens.

The day dreaded by many. The Cyber Day.

It is characterised by silence emanating from their child's room.

It is silent, apart from the occasional laugh.

And the whirring of the computer.

It is also characterised by what adults call 'anti-social behaviour'.

Teens call it 'keeping them occupied'.

Adults never know what is happening on the screen to captivate their child.

Words are screamed out of the room, strange mysterious words.

What is a Fan-Girl?

Is it a cult?

What kind of feels, are they talking about?

All they know is that supper is cut short by rushing from the table.

By the next day everything is back to normal.

Till the next Cyber Day

DAISY CHAIN

I loved the simplicity of it.

I admired the beauty of it.

It is formed so easily.

It is so natural.

You hated the difficulty of it, how fragile it was.

How it could break at any moment.

It leaves all that effort for nothing.

But now that chain is broken, it is smashed upon the floor.

What was once there, is not there anymore.

I remember the daisy chains, we made when we were young.

I see the crowd around the box.

They are all dressed in little black frocks.

I see tears enter every eye.

I feel a tear enter mine.

I watched the soul rise, though the grey granite sky.

I waited in a bed when I knew.

I thought about my first funeral.

It was a ceremony of grief and woe.

It is a kind of morbid show.

A demonstration of death, for all those left.

FAIRY RING

My father said there was a fairy ring.

It's up upon the hill, beside the burial of the old elfin king.

I visited it every day untill...

I visited it in rain and I visited it in snow.

I wanted to see the Fae.

It was well after dark when I would go.

I realised one day.

I realised fairies are not there.

What I believe no longer includes those masters of the air.

I only believe in things that are real.

FORM TIME

It is the beginning of the school day.

You hear the chattering of tiny birds.

Though it's just the talk of tiny humans.

There are the groups of friends making jokes about nothing.

You walk to your friends nattering.

The teacher yells "Please settle down!"

As a bunch of people are pretending to moo like a cow.

The teacher takes roll call.

"Zoë, Molly, Abbie,"

"Present" we all chorus one by one.

As we set off to double English.

There is a reason my favourite time is form time.

FIRST SNOW

It was the first snowfall of the year and he was freezing.
He watched the snowy wood and sat there in the cold and the glorious silence.

He hated being at home sometimes.
He hated when his parents went on raging, arguing and blaming.

So he would just sit here and sit until he thought it was safe.
Not even the snow could keep him away from his spot when they started to argue.

His brother wasn't here.
He had escaped.
Sometimes he even hated his brother for that.
But all he needed was this place.
Just to be able to be alone and to be able to think.

It was time to go back now.
They would have finished about now.
He got up from the bench he was sitting on and took a final look at the white flakes of show.

Some people used to believe that snow was Gods frozen tears.
He could believe that, if humans can get so sentimental than why not God.
So he walked back in the direction of the house.
He walked from ice into fire.

Dreams flick through my soul.

Full of secrets never told, of flaws, jaws and claws.

Dreams full of pain, blood and mud.

Full of gunshots.

I wake up pale and numb.

Dreaming of battles to come.

MY FRIENDSHIP

Our shopping trips to town.

Toilet paper made into a crown.

Late night games of truth or dare.

Truths so secret we have to swear.

Bets are made all in jest.

Memories I put in my minds treasure chest.

We laugh and laugh until we lose our breath.

Talking about things we never left.

Our phones by our side, we have our fun.

MY PHONE

You are my constant companion.

.

You hold all my secrets, in one form or another.

You know me well, you know me sad.

You entertain me when I am bored.

You suck me into your cyber world.

And then you spit me out.

You are the unattached limb to my body.

You are so breakable like bones.

You are Mercury going across the skies to deliver my message.

Yet I fear that part of my soul is no longer in my head.

The town burned, fire lighting up the midnight sky.
My mind delved into the depth of the flames.
The flickering sun beams etching and burning across the suburban landscape.

Buildings crumbled into the ash from which they came.
Pockets of ruby flames flickered in the landscape like little jewels.
Little jewels causing chaos.

It was days before the whole fire was smothered.
My legacy etched on to the hill where the town used to be.
My mark upon the landscape, there will always be ash and soot there now.

I'm quite proud of that.

You ask why I did it.
I suppose it was my parents smiling at me.
They didn't believe me.
They didn't believe I needed help.
I would prove them wrong.

It was easy you know.
It was bonfire night.
Just add a few extra things into the bonfire.
Then watch the beautiful chemical cocktail ignite.

The town burned.
Like hell had opened up to greet me, and I welcomed it

I said I would prove them wrong.

I am heartless.

 I am cruel.

I am no one's fool.

I am not lonely or forgotten

I just delight at being rotten.

I am not weak.

 I am strong.

Everyone else is wrong.

I just need myself.

 I do not need any help

I do not cry every night,

 As normal people might.

I do not need a friend, for me to mend

TO A GHOST

I see her in front of me.

She is as pale as the clouds, thin as a stick.

Your eyes have no soul.

They are black like an abyss.

I see the ivory bones beneath the skin.

They are as brittle as a twig.

Her hair is thin like spider webs.

They cling desperately around her head.

I look on unhappily.

As I try to look at the refection of me.

A ghost of what I used to be.

Just a ghost.

Thud, thud across the pitch.

Suspense builds around.

The Crowd grows quiet.

Shh......

We line up, looking at each other.

One of us is going to win.

The shrieking whistle whirls.

I run.

The wind is whistling through my hair.

I'm floating on the air.

I run past the finishing line.

The crowd roars with support.

I wake up, and get ready.

I am going to win this sports day.

OUR ACTIONS

We think our actions do not have consequences.

They do.

All your decisions are connected to other people's decisions.

Like a giant's spider web which affects not only the present but the future.

Down to the tiniest decision like where to eat for lunch.

You eat at a tiny family shop.

So they have food to eat.

You are kind to someone.

So they kind to those they meet.

It is a chain of events which shifts the universe slightly with every decision.

Every mortal makes an influence on this earth.

However small it is.

Everybody's decisions impacts everybody else.

They affect you.

ALONE

That is what we fear the most isn't it?

We fear being alone.

We fear going from cradle to grave alone.

So we lie.

We pretend what we are not.

We become who are not.

But that's wrong.

Because we are never alone, you just have to look around.
Just reach out for company.
Drop the mask of self-pretence.
Walk out of the shadows.
Then join the company.
We are all afraid of being alone.

MAYBE

We make mistakes.
Things we know are wrong.
Not everyone has what it takes, to say as clearly as a brass gong.

 Maybe I was wrong.

In the dead of midnight if you look.

You might be surprise at what you find.

You see a young girl on their bed.

A laptop is in her hand.

There are many things they could do on a laptop at this time.

Maybe watch a movie, watch a bit of TV.

Trail though Google, watch an Anime.

Maybe read a Manga or tour Tumblr.

Maybe a few midnight tweets on Twitter.

This poor young girl just can't decide.

So she decides to do them all.

The endless possibilities turn into endless hours.

Her mind starts to blur.

She wakes up at 11 AM her laptop still on.

It was a good night.

IT WILL NOT HAPPEN

Children are told when they are young.

"One day little girl, you will grow up."

Among the years of carefree innocence you don't believe it.

Luck will not permit you so; you will stay young and fit.

Then Pandora's Box is opened.

Innocence has gone.

You find fear and responsibility in her stead.

Steadily go where everyone is led.

To the strange land of adulthood I will go.

Where she will be untill she finally rests.

FRIDAY

The bells ring for the final time.
They start to run.
Running away or running to?
I never know.

They leave behind their books and sums.
They leave behind the stuffy classrooms and the musk smell.
They get to get away.
Well ok, until the Sunday marking gets underway.

?

SUMMER DAYS

Summer is a time of fun.

Isn't it?

Blissful days summer sun.

Swimming pools full with watery fun.

Endless days, mindless and bored.

So very bored.

You stay in bed.

You have nowhere to go.

Your friends are away.

You have nowhere to go.

You occupy yourself.

But it's not the same.

So don't blame me for wanting school again?

PARENT PLOT

Your parents are plotting again.

You see it in their eyes.

You hear it in the mutterings in the kitchen.

You feel it in the air.

You taste it in the decrease mum's cooking.

They are plotting your downfall.

You know it.

But there is nothing you can do.

 So you let it happen.

You expect it when they asking you to sit down.

But you know you have to.

So you sit down.

Their lips open.

"We're going to move again."

I told you so.

CHRISTMAS DAY

The bells across the windows, beckon Christmas day.

Children run down the stairs.

Clatter, clatter down the stairs.

Clatter, clatter down the stairs.

The excitement is in the air.

Magic too.

So much so the adults feel it too.

Even though they are woken by children running down the stairs.

With the thud, thud of the children going downstairs.

With the thud, thud of the children going downstairs.

The family is gathered all around after the affectionate bicker during Christmas Lunch.

It still unites them and they tie together, one and all.

It is Christmas anyway.

It is Christmas anyway.

The smoke gives a delightful bliss.

I fall.

Fall into this blanket of content.

Everything is just fine.

Everything is well.

This content fills my body, reaching every crevice.

I need this bliss.

My body craves and welcomes it.

Everything is just fine.

Everything is well.

The world passes me, I let it pass me.

I pity their worries.

I am beyond that now.

Everything is just fine.

Everything is well.

I am the metaphorical Alice, I'm in Wonderland now.

I'm going into the rabbit hole.

I'm falling forever.

Everything is just fine.

Everything is well.

PRIZE GIVING

Prize giving is the doom of everybody.

Children either anticipate it or dread it.

The desire for a prize is fire in their eyes.

The bitter loss of a prize poisons them against it.

But they should rejoice in collective achievements.

Not resent individual achievements.

Teachers can't stand it.

First there is the choice of who to pick.

Not everyone can win a prize.

Then there is the order that must be kept.

There is a pressure to show the school at its best.

The headmistress loves it.

She stands up to speak.

She sees her children row on row.

She shows off her children's achievements.

See how well they have done.

But in one way or another they are all pleased when they leave that day.

SIZE

"What size are you?"

"Oh I'm a size..."

"Really you're really that size."

"Yes."

"Oh, ok."

I hate when people obsess over size.

Does it really matter?

Is really important?

Apparently yes.

"Oh are you going to eat that?"

"No... I'm trying to watch my size."

People say they don't care but they do.

They always do.

I do too.

I hate myself for that.

BEAUTY

I want to be beautiful.

Everybody does.

It's a known fact.

Everyone wishes to be Aphrodite.

To be admired for their looks.

But there are different types of beauty.

You see it all around.

You see the smiles which makes them glow.

A laugh that makes them looks stunning.

In a weird little way.

Everyone is beautiful.

It just takes a while to realise.

Is she wrong, or bad?

She is she just guilty of naivety?

Is that her crime?

A young girl is pregnant, she is unwed.

Her parents may condemn her.

Her friends scorn her.

Her lover rejects her.

Under all she was desperate for love.

She is desperate to be wanted by someone.

She is desperate not to end up alone.

So she is unwise.

But is that a capital crime?

BLACK

Black is the colour of the night at its darkness.

Black is the clothes on a thief who is trying not to be noticed.

Black is the colour of unlucky cats which you step across.

Black is the colour of hole which seems bottomless.

Black is the colour of your mind at its darkest.

But in the blackness there is always light.

The dawn comes at the end of the dark night.

Food is in the mouths of the children of the unnoticed thief.

Unluckiness is in you, not a cat.

There is a bottom to the hole.

And when your mind is black?

There is someone to bring you back into the light.

ROSE PETALS

The Rose is the symbol of love.

It is the never ending symbol.

It stays whether the rose is as ruby red as blood.

Or the rose alabaster, white as a dove.

The rose's thorns are so harsh that soft fingers need a thimble.

It grows in fertile soil up to the sky.

Curling, creeping, choking around the wooden cane.

But still a rose can wither and die.

Or grow wild so they will never be tamed.

Rose petals can be poisoned, turn ugly inside.

FAMILY

It is the warmth of comfort surrounding me.

It nurtures and secures me.

We may bicker and quarrel.

But they are still there.

They have an everlasting effect on you.

Whatever form of family it may be.

Homework is the devils work.

Sitting there waiting to be done.

It is the ultimate judge.

It is the lion you try to tackle.

It is the job you have to do.

You glare at it from the other side of the table.

It peeks out of the bag expectently.

You take it out cautiously, waiting for it to bite.

You open it and start the marathon.

Writing, writing, writing....

Then it's done...

It's done.

The euphoria washes over you.

You strut back to the bag

You see another book of homework to do inside

THE GRADUATION

The pupils arrive there line in line.

Hugs exchanged before they go inside.

They sit down smiling in anticipation.

The stage is set.

It begins.

Mothers cry one and all.

Their little ones have left the nests.

When it's over everyone cries.

Phone numbers exchanged.

"We must keep in touch."

Most they will never see again.

Never ever again will you see their faces.

Then they are left with something empty inside.

They know not what it is.

As they move on to the next stage, line in line.

The English class starts.

We are all set at full attention.

We are explorers, exploring literature.

We go from Frost to Duffy, Hardy to Dickinson.

We go from God like sun to bitter snow.

We go from heroes to detectives in the blink of an eye.

We see pain, we see mourning, and we see people going mad.

But most I think we see hope, the writers hope for humanity and its hopeless ways.

Then we are back in the blink of eye.

We return to the day.

Out the classroom we all go.

"That's not healthy."

"That is an unhealthy outlook."

"That is not a healthy situation."

We constantly told what is unhealthy for us.

But what is healthy?

There is mentally healthy.

Knowing your mind ticks.

Not being afraid of what is in your mind.

Not letting the darkness creep into your perfectly functioning mind.

That's healthy?

There is also physical healthiness.

The ability to run, jump and dance.

Not seeing any imperfection on your skin that you would change.

Not eating anything not good for you.

That's healthy?

Or not being ill.

Never having a cough or a cold?

Never having to go to the doctors?

Is that healthy?

Because it seems that anyone who worries about being healthy is unhealthy.

I am lying here in darkness.

There is no light.

No feeling too.

I am numb.

I don't care anymore.

I am just content floating.

Floating, floating.

I am just floating in my own little dark world.

Here, no one can touch me.

No one can even try.

They might be there somewhere but...

Not now.

Suddenly light irrupts above me.

You see flashing crimson, emerald and violet light.

The light surrounds me.

Feeling returns to my body.

My very own Aurora Borealis.

My Northern Lights.

FOR THE LAST TIME

Everything could be for the last time.

You just never know.

It could be something silly like the last time you read a book.

It's still the last time though.

Then you have more serious types of last times.

The last time you see a pet.

The last time you see a friend.

The last time you catch a breath.

The world is full of last times

But it is also full of first times.

You see the person in front of you.

She is mocking you.

She is smirking knowingly.

She knows you all too well.

She is disgusted by you.

She is always disappointed in you.

You just want to knock that disappointment of her face.

So you do.

You strike her.

 Your hatred shows.

Crash....

The broken pieces of glass cover the floor.

A FLICKERING LIGHT

A flickering light that is always bright.

It lies within deep within my skin.

When I am kicked and feel a punch it doesn't hurt much.

But still my light did nothing but shine, my own little shrine.

But you saw that, and decided to attack.

You squash that light with all your might.

You left me in the dark leaving your mark.

Now I struggle to turn on the flickering light.

I try to bring back its old delight.

But it's gone.

It's hard letting go.

Especially hard is letting go in a fight.

It seems like you are a coward.

Just let it go.

It is hard of let go of something which you feeling guilty about

It is like a worm wriggling inside you.

It is waiting to come out.

Just let it go.

It is hard letting go of fears.

They follow you everywhere.

They are present in your tears.

Just let it go.

Just let it go.

Think no more and live your life.

If guilt, fear and cruelty return.

Just say, "No."

MISTAKEN

I made a mistake.

Now it's too late.

I just have to wait.

Minutes go by.

I'm going to die.

Blood trickles and pours from my hands.

A QUESTION

Have you realised that everything which changes in your life starts with a question?

What question?

I don't know.

Do you?

A question to yourself.

A question to another.

A question asked.

Every change starts with a question.

If you think about how important a question is.

Think about how important the answer is.

Lies pollute this earth.

They float around grinning at you.

You never know when one will pounce on you.

You never know when it is doing so.

You see an angel smiling at you.

You don't see the animal attacking you.

MISUNDERSTOOD

People never see me clearly.

They have a tinted glass when they pass by.

They don't like the view.

So they don't look again.

People like me are never seen clearly.

Children are groomed with preconceptions.

Those preconceptions make them pass me by.

I wish they wouldn't.

DEATH PENALTY

I walk across the street.

I see a boy getting beating up.

I see his head swing side to side with every punch.

I see his neck batted and bruised.

I see his breath escape at last.

I go back in time.

I see a boy being hung.

I see him swing side to side with swing of the rope.

I see his neck battered and bruised.

I see his breath escape at last.

There is more than one way to receive the death penalty.

JUST AN OUTCAST

I see them laugh.

As they see me cry.

I walk away.

I try console myself.

I'm just an outcast.

Just don't care.

Teacher looks disappointed in me.

Saying she have to call my family.

I just nod my head.

I try console myself.

I'm just an outcast.

Just don't care.

I see my father shouting at me.

He slaps me hard for all to see.

Ignore the pain.

I try console myself.

I'm just an outcast.

Just don't care.

THE DREADED PHONE CALL

You knew it was coming.

That phone call.

It was evitable as the setting sun.

As foreseeable as the tide

As predictable as pain and loss.

That was how certain it was.

It rings clearly as a bell.

Just as clearly as a telephone.

You look at the number.

It's that phone call all right.

Your heart picks up its beat.

As you pick up the phone.

Some things will never be forgotten.

You will see it in your head.

You taste the memories of nourishment long past its sell by date.

You hear in the echoes of your past.

You feel sensations which slip through your fingers.

You smell aromas flooding from your past.

Some things will never be forgotten.

LIGHTENING STRIKES AGAIN

You stole once.

Only once.

You regretted it.

You felt the disappointment.

You heard the whispers.

You felt the handcuffs go one.

You have tasted the rotten prison gruel.

You paid your time.

You said you never do it again.

Lighting never strikes twice

You walk past a street a year later.

The object of desire flicks across your eyes.

You feel the longing for it.

You can't let it slide.

You decide.

You wish that lighting never struck again.

Time stops for no man.

He is running.

It doesn't want to slow down like us mortals.

He is running against the old grandfather Clock.

He is afraid that we will catch up with it.

He sees the pain in our eyes.

So he never stops.

That pain, he wants none of it.

Never knowing he was the cause of it.

A FLASH OF HOPE

You walk out. You are tired.

You are alone.

You have run away from home.

You grip your coat oh so tight,

To keep out the snapping frostbite.

Someone emerges from his front door.

He walks to you.

You cower in fear.

What is he going to do to you?

He passes you a bag,

Then walks away.

You look in and see a treasure trove.

I see a blanket, a flashlight and a bundle of food.

A flash of hope illuminates the dark night.

A GIRLS NIGHT OUT

Girls flock together.

They fly side by side.

They laugh together...

They cry together.

And they sure as hell go out together.

They chink their drink in good luck.

Then they hit the dance floor.

Guys are circling around the room.

But they have each other's back.

One gets so drunk she starts spouting secrets,

One is so drunk you can see it in her dance moves.

One is so drunk she gives a stranger her number.

One is so sober she rips it from his hand.

She is also the one who leads the flock home.

But all in all it was a good girl's night out.

Falling in love for the first time is like a car heading straight for you.

It is blindingly unexpected.

It is like tattooing your body.

It has an everlasting effect.

It is like not having the biggest toy in the playground.

It leaves you jealous and annoyed.

It is like a band playing outside your window.

It keeps you awake at night.

It is like writing in permanent marker.

It never truly goes.

But then again all this could be said for every time you fall in love.

THE ACCIDENT

It was accident.

I swear it was.

But it's done now

No, I never meant to do it.

You have to believe me.

There was nothing I could do.

CITY

It is a maze to be lost in.

A high tech, Skyscraper maze.

The maze though contains thing you could only dream off.

Vivid colours of the rainbow surround you.

As you view the crowd also trapped in this maze.

Glitz and glamour glitter through shop windows

So it leaves you in a state of joyful confusion.

It is very disconcerting.

COUNTRYSIDE

It is like a museum.

No internet!

No Wi-Fi!

Just fields!

But I see still the beauty roll for on miles and miles.

I heard the birds cheerfully chirp, music to my ears.

I smell the grass newly mown.

I taste the yeast in the air on my tongue.

I suppose I could get used to this.

STORY TIME

I used to love story time.

Tales of dragons, fairies and mermaids.

Of courage, bravery and valour.

The hero was dashing.

The heroine was beautiful.

Magic was all around.

But lately I find,

I cannot take solace in these tales.

I start myself thinking.

Of much darker tales

GROW TO CARE

We are born not caring.

We are born selfish.

But then we grow to care.

We grow to feel empathy.

We grow to feel compassion.

We grow to feel guilty.

So if you shrug your shoulders.

Then tell me, "You don't care".

Well then, you're telling me a lie.

This lesson is torture.

It's not the teacher.

It's the course.

And the one and half hour lesson to teach it in.

The clock just goes so slowly.

I think it must be as boring to teach as to learn.

I suddenly have great compassion and respect for the teacher.

Printed in Great Britain
by Amazon